"Reading *DogSense: 99 Relationship Tips from Your Canine Companion* lifted my spirits and reminded me of how uncomplicated and unconditional love can be. As a human, we have so much to learn from our four-legged companions! This book should be in the "self-help" section."

**—Jamie Wolf**
guardian of many dogs and owner of
PetLover Central Doggy Day Care, Boca Raton, Florida

"*DogSense: 99 Relationship Tips from Your Canine Companion* puts on paper what my clients and patients have communicated verbally for years, which is "the human-animal bond is more than just having a pet, it's developing an emotional bond that is many times stronger than a human-human bond."

**—Dr. Scott O. Lund**
president of Lund Animal Hospital (*www.BocaVet.com*)

"*DogSense: 99 Relationship Tips from Your Canine Companion* makes perfect sense to me as a dog translator. Dogs give unconditional love and attention, and they show the utmost patience with humans. If we could take their advice, our human relationships would be on cloud nine."

**—Jill Deringer-Thimmins**
dog translator featured on the *Late Show with David Letterman*,
*The Ellen DeGeneres Show*, Steve Harvey's *Big Time Challenge*,
Animal Planet's *Pet Star* and *30 Seconds to Fame*

"Unlike most books about pets, *DogSense: 99 Relationship Tips from Your Canine Companion* is about the heart and soul of any significant relationship—unconditional love! As a psychotherapist, I occasionally recommend certain books to my patients for insights into their relationship problems. While not technically a self-help book, I am pleased to add *DogSense* to my short list of recommended readings."

**—Robert M. Pasen, Ph.D.**
President & CEO of Neurobehavioral
Health Connections Ltd., with offices in
Mundelein, Barrington, and Crystal Lake, Illinois

"*DogSense: 99 Relationship Tips from Your Canine Companion* is a must-read for dog owners who want to see the world through their pet's eyes. In my 25-plus years of investigating animal cruelty cases and seeing the suffering dogs must endure at the hands of their cruel owners, I found this book to be a refreshing side-step into the human-animal relationship and how dogs might perceive their humans."

**—Roy Gross**
Chief of Department, Suffolk County SPCA, Smithtown, New York

To my husband, Richard,
who has indulged my passion for dogs.
To my daughter, Laura, who has reluctantly
shared me with my dogs.
To Zack and Quincy, my current dogs,
as well as their predecessors, all of whom
have enriched my life.

**Library of Congress Cataloging-in-Publication Data**

Genender, Carla.
  Dogsense : 99 relationship tips from your canine companion / Carla Genender ;
with photographs by Amy Hill.
    p.  cm.
  ISBN 0-7573-0553-9 (trade paper)
  1. Dogs—Behavior.  2. Human-animal relationships.  I. Title.  II. Title: Dog sense.

SF433.G43  2006
636.7'0887—dc22

                                                                              2006028747

Publisher:
Health Communications, Inc.
3201 S.W. 15th Street
Deerfield Beach, Florida 33442-8190

*Photographs: ©2006 Amy Hill*
*Cover design by Larissa Hise Henoch*
*Inside book design by Larissa Hise Henoch*

# DogSense

## 99 Relationship Tips from Your Canine Companion

### Carla Genender
with photographs by Amy Hill

Foreword by Marty Becker, D.V.M.
Coauthor of *Chicken Soup for the Dog Lover's Soul*

**Health Communications, Inc.**
**Deerfield Beach, Florida**

*www.hcibooks.com*

# contents

# *Foreword*

The focus of my twenty-six-year career as a veterinarian, author, media personality and pet lover is the affection and connection between animals and people—which I call "The Bond." Pets are unique beings that have minds and personalities of their own, and they form strong bonds with their owners. This is true of all kinds of pets, but arguably none is closer than the human/dog bond.

If you've ever shared your life with a dog, you know that the human/dog bond exists and that you can count on your dog for acceptance rather than rejection, empathy rather than indifference, security rather than anxiety, companionship rather than loneliness, connection rather than separation and joy rather than heartbreak. You also know that dogs don't lie or cheat; they have to-die-for loyalty and love unconditionally.

I hope you enjoy *DogSense: 99 Relationship Tips from Your Canine Companion*. It is a celebration of the human/dog bond and an extension of that bond as a role model for human relationships. The photos will make you smile, and the tips can help you build stronger human/human bonds.

**Marty Becker, D.V.M.**
Author of *The Healing Power of Pets* and *Fitness Unleashed*
Coauthor of *Chicken Soup for the Dog Lover's Soul,*
*Why Do Dogs Drink Out of the Toilet?* and
*Do Cats Always Land on Their Feet?*
Resident veterinarian on ABC's *Good Morning America*

# Introduction

Dogs and humans have always had a special relationship: They give and receive unconditional love. Anyone who has ever had a relationship with a dog knows how affectionate, caring, appreciative, attentive, accepting and adept at communicating their feelings and desires they are. So, who better to learn from when seeking a role model for good relationships? This concept first came to me one night when I was annoyed with my husband. I wanted to talk to him about something, but he was preoccupied. In frustration, I told him that even our dogs listen better than he does.

The more I thought about it, the more I realized that there are other things our dogs do better than he does. For example, they are always happy to see me, they kiss and snuggle any chance they get and they are always willing to go with me when I ask. To be fair, I also realized that there are things the dogs do better than I do. I became intrigued with the idea that we humans could learn relationship skills from our dogs. Thus, this book was born.

As a former management consultant, I put my research skills to use and explored the body of information available about marital and relationship advice. Then I took the information and organized it—six categories emerged, and they became the six chapters of this book: Caring, Attention, Affection, Communication, Acceptance and Appreciation. The meaning of each category is represented by the quotes at the beginning of each chapter.

The photographs were taken by Amy Hill, a professional wedding photographer. I met Amy through the Art Institute of Fort Lauderdale. I chose her because the photos on her website are natural and joyful—two characteristics I wanted for the photos in the book. I also liked the idea of a wedding photographer taking the photos for a dog book about relationships!

Writing this book was a wonderful experience. I met many nice people, and I was especially rewarded by the fact that some of them let me know I had touched their lives. In some cases, it was because the dog was ill and being in this book became a tribute. In other cases, people told me how well the tips assigned to their dogs actually fit themselves and caused them to think about their own relationship issues. And some told me that the feelings expressed by the dogs about their owners really helped them at a low point in their lives.

The photos featured in *DogSense: 99 Relationship Tips from Your Canine Companion* will bring a smile to your face, while the dog biographies shed light on their diverse personalities and interests. Allow the relationship tips that accompany each photo to guide you gently through your daily interactions with the people you encounter. Most of all, enjoy it!

*Our love must not be a thing of words and fine talk. It must be a thing of action and sincerity.*

I John 3:18

# caring

*We give dogs time we can spare, space we can spare and love we can spare. And in return, dogs give us their all. It's the best deal man has ever made.*

M. Acklam

# Duke

## One-year-old Great Dane

I'm a big guy. This was apparently a surprise to my first family, because they told Great Dane Rescue that they didn't realize how large I would get. The rescue people helped me get adopted four times. I don't know why the first three didn't last—maybe because I tore up the grass when I ran, or maybe it was the dirt I brought inside. Anyway, the fourth home was a keeper. I have a great life with a retired couple, a female Great Dane as a companion, and three acres of fenced land where I can run free. I show my gratitude by assuming guard dog responsibilities.

*Although the name implies this breed came from Denmark, it actually originated in Germany, where it is known as the Deutsche Dogge, meaning German mastiff.*

*Protect her from danger.*

# Maggie

**Three-year-old cairn terrier**

My favorite activity is playing with the squirrels in my yard. Each morning I pick a squirrel to stare at. It seems to me that it comes closer and closer before it eventually scampers away. Then I find another squirrel and start all over again. My favorite person, out of the three wonderful people in my life, is my human brother. He's a very special guy who needs me more than anyone, and I'm drawn to that need. We have a bond that is incredibly strong, and I would do anything for him. When he's home, I stay at his side. When he's out, my heart is in his pocket.

*The breed comes from the Isle of Skye in Scotland where they hunted rats and other vermin. Cairns are heaps of stones found on the island, placed there as memorials or landmarks.*

4

Be his guardian angel.

# Nikita

## Seven-year-old schipperke

The German shepherd I live with is my polar opposite. She's a couch potato; I like to stay busy. She likes to be told what to do; I like to tell others what to do. When I want a belly rub, I climb on Mom's lap and roll over. If necessary, I use my paws to push her hand to the right spot. When I want a treat, I sit up and beg, and I usually get one. My favorite thing to do is surf in our pool. I stand by my surfboard until a family member holds it against the side of the pool so I can hop on.

*The breed was developed in Flanders as ratters on ships and for guarding canal barges. The name refers to the way they act in charge; in Flemish* schipperke *means little captain or skipper.*

*Take at least 15 minutes a day just for yourself.*

# Remington

## Six-year-old German shorthaired pointer

Life is very interesting in my house. There are three humans, me, my biological son, a hamster and a chinchilla. I enjoy playing with my son, but he can be annoying. Sometimes I have to put him in his place. One of the humans is a young female (my girl); I enjoy playing with her too, even though she can also be annoying. I'm very patient and tolerant, though, because she's little and doesn't know any better or mean any harm. The hamster and chinchilla are very intriguing. I love to sit in front of their cages and point at them—this seems to entertain my humans, especially my girl.

*The breed was developed in Germany at a time when average working people couldn't afford multiple specialized hunting dogs. These multitaskers can track, point and retrieve.*

*share child-care responsibilities.*

# Nick

## Ten-year-old Rhodesian ridgeback

I'm calm and easygoing except for two circumstances: when there's a thunderstorm, and when there's food around. I hate thunderstorms! I know it seems foolish for a big, strong guy like me, but they terrify me. I often become agitated during storms and chew on anything I can find. I'm ashamed to say that has included the couch (I ate a hole in it), the powder room wall (I ate a hole in it), and an area rug (I ate a corner of it). As much as I hate storms, I love food. My life revolves around food. I'm either eating, thinking about eating, or watching my humans eat and hoping they'll share.

*The breed was developed in Rhodesia. Ridgeback comes from the unusual ridge of fur that grows forward on its back.*

Help with the dishes.

# zack

## Eight-year-old Yorkshire terrier

My mom is the author of this book, so it's not surprising that she dressed me up to be photographed. She's always trying to get Dad to dress up too, but he'd rather be casual. I don't mind—actually, I think I look handsome. Yesterday I got groomed so I would look my best. The

*The breed is named for Yorkshire, England, where it originated.*

photo session took quite a while; the photographer kept trying out different locations to get the best setting and lighting. She couldn't believe how long I was willing to sit and pose. But I know it's important to Mom, and she does so many things to make me happy, it's my pleasure to make her happy.

Be willing to dress up if special occasions are important to her.

# Duffy

## Three-year-old Lhasa apso

My life revolves around Mom and Dad, who are the absolute best parents. When they go out, I hang out on our front

*Lhasa apsos come from Tibet and were named for the sacred city of Lhasa. The monks used them to guard temples and nicknamed them the Lion Dog of Tibet.*

porch, watching the world go by and waiting for them to come home. If I get tired or bored, I use my doggie door to go inside. At night I sit up, I roll over, and I give my paw just as I was taught; and for these wonderful performances (just as *I* taught *them*), I receive my favorite treats.

Oh yes, it's a dog's life, and I sure am happy! If they would only leave my teeth alone I would be even happier.

Take good care of your teeth; bad
breath is a turnoff.

# Maggie

**Two-year-old English setter**

I live with another English setter and two humans. It's a good life, a great life actually, but I wish there were children in the house. I'm a sucker for small dogs and children. With small dogs I lie down to be at eye level, so we can socialize. With children I also lie down, so they can pet me (and sometimes slip me some food). I love going outside because there are interesting smells and I have room to romp around. Sometimes we go hiking, which is even better than regular walks because we stay out much longer. I even have my own backpack!

*The breed name comes from its country of origin and from their use as bird hunters who would sit or "set" after locating their prey.*

*carry your own weight.*

# Miss Tyson Penelope

## Nickname Ty, seven-year-old boxer

My first home was with a swinging bachelor who bragged that I was a great babe magnet. When I was seven months old he gave me to Boxer Rescue—he said I was "no longer cute." This from a man who thought it was cute to name me Tyson (as in Mike Tyson) because I'm a boxer. What kind of name is that for a girl? My new family stole my heart when they said they didn't want me to go through the trauma of a new name, yet Tyson didn't seem feminine. So I became Miss Tyson Penelope. I try to be as concerned about their feelings as they are about mine.

*One theory about how boxers got their name is that when they fight, they stand on their hind legs and use their front paws in a boxing motion.*

*Dry her tears when she's sad.*

# Canton Alexandría II

## Nickname Ali, four-year-old chow chow

I lead a privileged life, and I love every aspect of it. My favorite hobby is going with my humans in our private plane, where I sit up front and act as co-pilot. Not many canines get this opportunity! When we're not on one of our frequent trips to the islands, we walk on the beach every afternoon. The sunsets are beautiful. I'm also fortunate that they take such good care of me; I have the kind of coat that would be matted if I didn't get brushed every day, especially with the humidity, sand and salty air. Thanks to my family I always look beautiful.

*This ancient Chinese breed was exported via ship, along with merchandise and food items. The captain wrote chow chow on the manifest instead of the different items, thus the breed name.*

*Look your best just for him.*

# Tyson

## Two-year-old Pekingese

I'm pretty much a couch potato. I know most canines enjoy long walks, but usually I just want to get my business done and go back inside. My favorite place to hang out is the ledge of our sofa because it gives me a great view. When Mom is home I like to spend my time cuddling with her. When I'm not feeling well, I limp around until she notices something is wrong. I always notice when Mom's not well—I stay even closer than usual to let her know I'm concerned.

*This breed originated in China and was named for Peking, the city that is now called Beijing.*

*Give her sympathy when
she's sick or hurt.*

# Princess

## Three-month-old Maltese

With a name like Princess, it's only natural to expect to be treated like one. And my humans meet my expectations. All

*In ancient times, the Maltese was considered an aristocrat among dogs and was valued for its beauty.*

I have to do is let them know when I want something. If I want to get up on Mom and Dad's bed, I sit next to it and make soft barks and they pick me up. If I want food, I scratch on the cabinet door where my food is kept and they give me food. If I want a belly rub, I roll onto my back near them and they rub my belly. When I want to go to sleep, I don't need any help for that; I just do it.

*Get plenty of rest
so you won't be cranky.*

# Eli

## Three-year-old goldendoodle

It's a good thing that I'm a very tolerant dog. If I weren't, I'd never make it in this family—the kids can really be a hand-

*The breed is a cross between a golden retriever and a standard poodle. It originated in the United States.*

ful! They pull my tail, tug my ears, grab my fur, tumble on me and, of course, dress me up. But it doesn't matter because I love them with all my heart, and I would do anything for them. I can't imagine a life without them; it would probably be very boring. Mom says I'm her hero for being so patient and understanding. Sometimes she calls me Nana, after Wendy's dog in *Peter Pan*.

Be her hero.

# sasha

## Five-year-old chocolate Labrador retriever

I'm lucky to live in a house with a pool, because I love to swim. My humans entertain a lot, and I always try to go for a swim when we have company—it's even more fun with an audience. But even if we didn't have a pool, I'd consider myself lucky. You see, I was adopted after being dropped off at a dog pound in the middle of the night. I do my best to get along and not cause any trouble. I never jump on people or steal food I could easily reach from counters and table tops (although sometimes it smells wonderfully tempting).

*Labrador retrievers have two features that help them retrieve waterfowl: webbed feet for more efficient swimming, and a tail similar to an otter's to help them turn in water.*

*Stay in shape. It makes you look and feel better.*

# Noel

## Sixteen-month-old hairless Chinese crested

I have the most amazing mom. She's an opera singer and former Broadway performer, and at bedtime she always sings a lullaby to me. Her voice is soothing and helps me relax. She even sings to me when we go to the vet to keep me from being nervous. It works! She talks to me all the time, too. Not only that, she talks and sings in English and Italian. I don't mean to brag, but I'm fluent in both. Mom has the most amazing costumes and stage jewelry, which she shares with me. Dad thinks it's hilarious when we play dress-up.

*Originally named the African hairless terrier, this breed was picked up by Chinese trading ships that stopped along the coast of Africa. They changed the name to Chinese crested.*

Dress up for him sometimes.

# Bailey

## Two-year-old Irish setter

I'm a gal who likes to be useful, so I go where the action is. We live on a golf course, and the action is often in the back-yard where the golf carts travel on the path outside our fence. I chase them to make sure they know not to trespass on our property. I also stay busy inside the house. During meal preparation and clean-up, I sit nearby, ready to take care of anything that spills on the floor. On laundry day, I take things out of the hamper if I can reach them. When I don't know how to help with work they're doing, I stay close and supervise.

*Irish refers to its country of origin; setter refers to the fact that they were bird hunters who pointed and then "set" while nets were thrown over the birds.*

Help with repairs around
the house.

## TJ

### Five-year-old mixed breed
### (mostly Labrador retriever)

I'm proud to be a certified service dog. It is my responsibility and my privilege to help Dad. He has multiple sclerosis, but doesn't let it stop him from leading a full life. Some of my responsibilities are to open doors for him, bring him his cane, open drawers and pick things up for him. I stay by his side at home and at work, ready to help whenever he needs me. Dad is very kind and appreciative; he doesn't get upset if I accidentally drop his cane or hand the wrong end to him. He also gives me a lot of affection, and I do the same for him.

*There are different types of service dogs. A dog that is the arms and legs for a disabled person is called a mobility assist dog.*

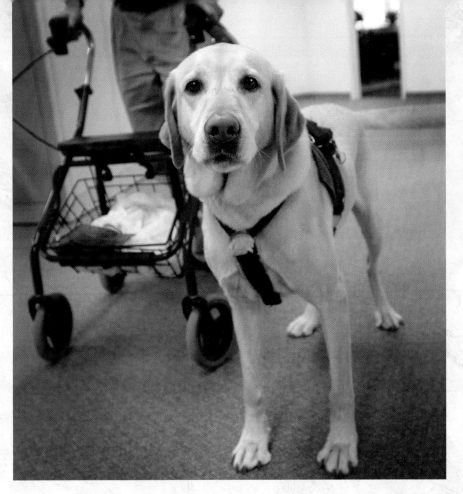

*Take on extra responsibilities
when you're needed.*

# Hailey

## Three-year-old American pit bull terrier

I have to confess that this photo is a bit misleading. I do believe in bringing gifts to show I care, but my gift of choice is usually a dead squirrel. It was the photographer's idea for me to pose with flowers instead. Even though I like to hunt squirrels and whatever other wild animals cross my path, I would never harm a person or another dog. Despite the reputation of my breed, I am very gentle when I play with my human and canine friends. I'm even gentle with my toys; I don't tear them up or chew holes in them.

*This breed is descended from bulldogs that were used to control unruly bulls for farmers and butchers. In the 1800s they were trained for the sport of dog fighting.*

*Bring her flowers for
no reason at all.*

*We've got this gift of love, but love is like a precious plant. You can't just accept it and leave it in the cupboard or just think it's going to get on by itself. You've got to keep watering it. You've got to really look after it and nurture it.*

John Lennon

## Attention

*You call to a dog and a dog will break its neck to get to you. Dogs just want to please.*

Lewis Grizzard

# Heide

## Five-year-old Doberman pinscher

I'm blessed with natural athletic ability. I enjoy developing and improving my talent, and my humans work with me regularly to prepare me for agility competitions. At first I was afraid to jump through obstacles, but now I'm fine with it. As a side benefit, my workouts keep me in good shape—an asset for a girl like me. The mere thought of losing muscle tone or gaining weight makes me shudder! When I'm not working out, I practice my nurturing skills with my many stuffed animals. Every night I bring them to bed, one by one; and every morning I take them back into the kitchen and play with them.

*The breed was developed in Germany by Louis Dobermann, a tax collector who traveled through dangerous areas and needed a dog to be a watchdog, a bodyguard and a companion.*

Be willing to jump through
hoops for him.

# Drifter

## Two-year-old whippet

I'm a former show dog, with emphasis on the word *former*. That life didn't suit me at all! It was very stressful, and there were way too many dogs. I know I'm a dog, but I prefer the company of humans. I'm glad I could retire at such a young age. When there's nothing going on, I'm happy to relax. If I get bored, I can always play with my toys, chew on a bone or look out the window. I do love to go outside. Walks are good—I just wish Dad wasn't so slow. Going to the park is even better, because I can go at my own (fast) pace.

*There are differing opinions as to how the breed got its name; one is that it comes from the whip-like tail.*

Be enthusiastic when he
asks you to join him.

# Quigley

## Two-year-old mixed breed

For some reason, humans always try to guess my origins; most think I look part Labrador retriever and part Weimaraner. I find this behavior odd. What would they think if I tried to guess the nationality of their children? I am uniquely me, a calm and friendly canine. I love to sit in the sun, play fetch, take long walks and wrestle with my canine friends. I don't like squirrels or any other species that threaten my domain. I am constantly on alert for the approach of these creatures; when one nears my territory, I bark to warn it away. I am equally sensitive to anything that might bother a family member.

*According to Margaret Bonham, author of* The Complete Guide to Mutts, *51 percent of pet-owning households in the United States have a mixed-breed dog.*

Try to sense trouble before it happens.

# cody

## Nine-year-old golden retriever

I had the honor of working at ground zero after 9/11, as one of the therapy dogs who comforted the first responders. It was a difficult time emotionally and physically. But my job was easy compared to the rescue dogs' job. Every hour they had to be given IVs for hydration and baths so they could continue their scent work. Sometimes a police officer would hide in the rubble just so the dogs could have a find—this kept them from getting discouraged. I'm still a therapy dog; Dad and I work for the Suffolk County SPCA in New York. When we're not working, we enjoy biking together.

*This is a Scottish breed, named for its golden coat and its use in hunting.*

*Get involved in a hobby
you enjoy together.*

# Rajah

## Nine-month-old Alaskan husky

I am a very intense dog. I have definite likes and dislikes: I like to play with other animals, even cats. I like being outside; my favorite outdoor activity is digging holes. I do not like water or food that isn't fresh; after my water and food have been out for more than three hours, I will not touch them. Fortunately my family is good about getting me fresh supplies. I do not like to be ignored. When I want attention, I stare at a family member. I am also careful not to ignore others; when a family member is talking to me or petting me, I tune everything else out.

*The Alaskan husky isn't an official breed. It originated in Alaska and was developed from Siberian huskies along with Alaskan malamutes and possibly other breeds, including Dobermans and greyhounds.*

*Give her your undivided attention.*

# Dougie

## Eighteen-month-old Cavalier King Charles spaniel

Unlike most canines, my breed never had a working func-
tion; we were only meant to provide companionship. I pride
myself on doing it well. However,
my humans lead busy lives. When
there's no one home, I'm at a loss—
how can I provide companionship
without a companion? When Dad
is home, I follow him everywhere:
If he stands, I sit at his feet; if he
sits down, I sit in his lap. I do have some hobbies of my
own. I enjoy chasing birds and playing with my best friend,
a beagle who lives next door.

*The breed is named for King
Charles II, who owned them
from the time he was a child
and, even as a ruler, was
rarely seen without two or
three dogs at his heels.*

*Sometimes he just needs
you to be there for him.*

# Tuxedo

## Nickname Zedo, twelve-year-old border collie

I may have less energy than I once had and I may sleep more, but when I see my Frisbee I'm ready for action. Mom and I have played this game since I was a puppy. Unless it's thrown really poorly, I almost always catch it. Life isn't all resting and playing for a working breed like me though. I have the self-appointed task of herding our ferrets. They live in very elaborate cages, but are often given free run in our screened-in porch. I watch to make sure they don't go into the house. I also help get them back in their cages when Mom tells them it's time.

*Border collies originated in the border country between England and Scotland where the terrain was rough; they had to be able to work independently and to reason.*

*Play together.*

# Baelyn

## Seven-year-old Yorkshire terrier

I am known to be quite the lover boy, very affectionate and demonstrative. I'm also quite laid back, until someone or something threatens my family, which consists of two humans and a female toy fox terrier who is afraid of her own shadow. If there is a stranger about (human or canine), I turn into a big dog with a ferocious bark. If someone is hurt, I use my tongue to soothe the pain. If someone is upset, I rub against them until they calm down. I'm sure that once they realize I'm on the job, they relax, knowing they are in good hands—or paws.

*Yorkshire terriers were originally owned by the working class in England. They were used as ratters; it was their job to protect small children from being bitten by rats at night.*

when she has a crisis, stay calm
and help put out the fire.

# Rascal

## Six-year-old papillon

When I was adopted from the Tri-County Humane Society in Boca Raton, Florida, I was undernourished, injured and skittish. I really lucked out with my new family—because of them, every day is a celebration! My favorite things to do are play and eat, and I've found a way to combine the two. When I'm fed, I first push my ceramic dish around the room (I'm careful not to break it). This is fun because it makes a lot of noise. After I get bored with moving the dish around, I take out one piece of food at a time, toss it in the air, bark at it and then eat it.

*The name of this French breed comes from the fact that their large erect ears are set on the high side of the head and fringed, resembling a butterfly. Papillon is French for butterfly.*

Remember to celebrate
important occasions.

# Buddy

## Four-year-old Siberian husky

I love cold weather, and what they call cold here in Florida doesn't do it for me; after all, my grandfather was a sled dog. Thank goodness for air conditioning. I try to stay cool by hanging out near the vents, preferably in the tiled areas of our house rather than on the carpets. When I'm not overheated, I'm actually quite frisky. I like exercise, whether it's playing tug-of-war or fetch or stretching my legs by running around a bit. I also like to go places with Mom. She can't take me to work, but during the weekends we usually hang out together.

*The breed originated in Siberia, hence the first part of the breed name. The second part of the name comes from "eskie," the old nickname for Eskimos, to whom these dogs belonged.*

Have a regular date night
for just the two of you

# Sasha

## Three-year-old Pomeranian

In addition to my humans, I share my home with a large mixed breed, mostly rottweiler I would guess. We were both adopted from the Palm Beach County Humane Society. We get along great because he accepts that I'm entitled to special privileges. I don't know if it's because of my size or because I flirt with him, but the reason isn't important. My privileges include being allowed on the furniture, being able to eat at a leisurely pace without worrying that he will steal my food, and going places while he stays at home. Sometimes I'd actually rather stay home, but I'd never hurt Dad's feelings by letting him know that.

*The breed is named for the area called Pomerania on the southern coast of the Baltic Sea (now Germany and Poland), from which it comes.*

Give a gift of your time;
join him in one of his hobbies,
even if it isn't your favorite.

# Bentley

## Eighteen-month-old bull terrier

Our house is on the beach of the Atlantic Ocean, so we can pretty much get away from it all whenever we want. We often walk on the beach, where I pick up coconuts, shred the shells until the coconut ball is left, and then play with it. After the beach I stand on the first step in the pool to rinse the sand off my paws. I can't stand that gritty feeling! Life isn't all fun and games though; it's my daily chore to go out and get the newspaper. When I bring it inside, I get my favorite treat—carrot sticks.

*This breed was created in England by crossbreeding the bulldog and the white English terrier, a now-extinct breed. They were originally called bull and terrier, then bull terrier.*

*Get away from it all*
*to have some alone time with her.*

# Austin

## Four-year-old Weimaraner

My sister and I live in a very active home. There's Mom, Dad, five-year-old twin boys and a nanny. With so many people I can usually find someone to play my favorite game: fetch. I like to keep it interesting, so sometimes I bring back what is thrown to me, and sometimes I hold onto it. I'm always gentle, though, especially with the twins. I hope to have twins (or more) of my own soon. I come from champion bloodlines, and I recently was introduced to a beautiful Weimaraner from equally good, but different, bloodlines.

*The breed originated in Germany, where it was first seen in the court of Weimar.*

*Make him laugh*
*when he's feeling down.*

# zachary

## Six-year-old Havanese terrier

I was adopted from the Humane Society of Broward County in Fort Lauderdale, Florida. I make it a point not to discuss my life before I arrived at the shelter, but I will say that as a result of my previous experiences I had what Mom calls "issues." No one could have been more kind, patient or understanding. I'm not exaggerating when I say she saved my life. I would do anything for her. Sometimes that includes going to some pretty boring places while Mom gets things done, but Dad's away a lot so I'm happy to fill in as her escort.

*This is the only breed native to Cuba. It is named after Havana, the capital.*

*Keep her company when*
*she runs errands.*

*clue*

## Eighteen-month-old American bloodhound

I have a very meaningful and fulfilling job working for the Palm Beach County sheriff's department: I help find missing people. I was donated by the Jimmy Rice Foundation, with the stipulation that I get extra training in finding lost children and that I be available whenever there's a lost child in my area. In my young career I have already found a missing child and a lost Alzheimer's patient. There is no way to describe the emotions when we have a successful find! I work with an incredible human partner. Between assignments, he helps me improve my tracking skills. When I'm off-duty, I live with him and his family.

*The breed got its name in England, when it was popular with British royalty and society. Because they were associated with "bluebloods," the breed became known as the bloodhound.*

*work as a team.*

*Talk not of wasted affection; affection never was wasted.*

Henry Wadsworth Longfellow

*Affection*

*Nobody can fully understand the meaning of love until he's owned a dog. He can show you more honest affection with a flick of his tail than a man can gather through a lifetime of handshakes.*

Author unknown

# colby

## Fifteen-year-old Australian shepherd

As I've gotten older I've lost some of my energy. I used to love to chase rabbits; now I only chase them in my dreams.

But with age has come wisdom. I now know that what matters most is spending time with the one I love and being close to her. When she pets me, there's nothing better—although taking a nap, going on a walk or getting a snack of peanut butter is pretty great, too. I'm sick now, and I know how sad it makes Mom. When the time comes that I have to leave her, I hope she is comforted by the memory of our wonderful years together.

*The Australian shepherd did not originate in Australia. It was actually developed in the United States, for the purpose of herding sheep imported from Australia.*

Let her hug you.

# Bugsy

## Four-month-old French mastiff

My normal day consists of waking up late, getting my belly rubbed, playing with friends, and sitting on the patio to soak up some sun while watching the world go by. When I get tired, I like to curl up next to Mom, put my head on her leg and take a nap. She says my big jowls spread out everywhere. My favorite nickname is Bugga Wugga. Mom says it with such love in her voice that I wag my tail like crazy. My heart fills with such love for her that I just stare at her and hope she can tell how I feel.

*The breed was valued by the French nobility before the French Revolution. Another name for this breed is Dogue de Bordeaux.*

Look at her with love in your eyes.

# Princess

## Four-year-old maltipoo

I was adopted from the Tri-County Humane Society in Boca Raton, Florida, when I was 18 months old. I have a wonderful home that I share with two other rescued canines, Marble and Cuddles. I crave human affection: kissing, cuddling, being held and sleeping curled up against Dad's legs at night. I enjoy going for a walk; when I see my leash, I get so excited I grab my yellow duck and shake it. I also like to play with my canine companions, especially Marble (a greyhound). I stand on my hind legs and smack her with my paw, then run. When Marble chases me, Cuddles tries to get in the middle to make us stop.

*A maltipoo is a hybrid between a Maltese and a poodle.*

*show pleasure when he holds you.*

# Maggie

## Five-year-old soft-coated wheaten terrier

I truly believe I was meant to be a small dog. I used to be small, and I assumed I would stay that way. It's hard to adjust! For example, I've always loved to jump on family members whenever they sit or lie down. Then one day, out of the blue, Mom made a funny sound when I landed on her, sort of like air coming out of a balloon. I jumped off and tried to run under a chair, but I got stuck and it turned over. Mom yelled. I hung my head down to say I was sorry. Mom said she was sorry for yelling.

*The breed comes from Ireland; the name refers to its soft coat that is the color of wheat.*

*Make up whenever you fight.*

## Cazanova

### Nickname Nova, ten-month-old miniature white schnauzer

Is this a great picture or what? I absolutely love it when Mom cuddles with me. I get a sense of peace that I remember having with my birth mom and my litter-mates. I am a bit concerned about this important aspect of our relationship though, because a man has entered Mom's life. I think he may be "the man" for her.

*Miniature schnauzers originally came from Germany. Schnauzer is German for whiskered snout.*

He's actually a great guy, but they do a lot of cuddling that doesn't include me! I do my best to wiggle my way between them. Sometimes they laugh; sometimes they move me out of their way. Needless to say, being excluded does not please me.

*cuddle often; it brings
you closer together.*

# Daisy

## Five-year-old rat terrier

My two favorite activities are chasing lizards and getting dressed up in one of my many outfits. But not at the same time—it's hard to run in clothes. I used to share my home with two humans; now they live apart and I spend weekdays with one and weekends with the other. At first I

*Rat terriers are an American breed created by early immigrants for farm and ranch work.*

hated it because I didn't understand what was happening and because they were both upset. But now we have all adjusted. I feel lucky that they are both still in my life, and I try to find ways to show each of them how much I care.

Find creative ways to
say "I love you."

# Shaina

## Five-year-old Maltese

My humans say I'm the world's best kisser. They also say I'm moody. I know I'm a good kisser—it's my favorite activity! I also enjoy barking and eating. But I'm not moody, except sometimes when other dogs board at our house. If I bark, they copy me and it gets so noisy that we all have to be quiet. Eating habits also change during these times; instead of having food available to eat whenever I want, I have access to food only at certain times. If I get miffed about the barking or eating restrictions, I have good reason! Thankfully our canine guests don't interfere with my daily kisses.

*This ancient breed came from the island of Malta, for which it is named.*

*Show your love every day.*

## Emma

### Nine-year-old greyhound

I started out as a racing dog, but they didn't think I had potential so I was given to Greyhound Rescue when I was still a youngster. I had a hard time calming down and getting over my panic at being separated from the other dogs. Once I got through the adjustment period, Mom entered my life. Being with her is way better than being with all my canine companions, and the accommodations sure beat those at the track! I don't like to be separated from her, and when she's home I stay close: kissing, getting pets, sitting in her lap or just lying next to her.

*Greyhounds were bred for hunting, and were known as sight hounds due to their keen eyesight. The name probably comes from the Old English* grighund, *which means dog hunter.*

*Enjoy the peaceful feeling that comes from being close to her.*

# Gunner

## Ten-year-old vizsla

Don't let my canine-like appearance fool you; I am 100-percent human. I like to go kayaking with family members, I lie on a swim float in the pool, and I can even skateboard a short distance by myself. I do not like to be separated from family members; when someone leaves

*This Hungarian breed's name means pointer; it is also known as the Hungarian pointer.*

the group I bark and spin 360 degrees in the air to protest. If a family member is eating something I want, I beg by putting my face in their lap and looking cute. I love to be petted, especially behind my ears and on top of my head; I make faces and noises to say it feels good.

*Let him know what*
*feels good to you.*

# Midnight

## Fourteen-month-old flat-coated retriever

My name refers to my fur color, but it suits me. Midnight is mysterious, and my family says that my licking fetish is a mystery to them. I lick people, other dogs, the floor, the furniture, the walls, my toys, shoes, etc. Midnight is bewitching, which I try to be when I want attention: I perform a series of tricks without being asked and hope someone notices. Midnight is when everything changes, and I like change. I can be obsessed with a toy one day and ignore it the next (usually after removing its squeaker). But one thing that never changes is that I enthusiastically greet everyone who enters our home.

*The breed was developed in England. The flat coat enables the dog to retrieve in bushy land areas; it is also more water resistant for retrieving in marshy water.*

*show you're glad to see her, even if she's only been gone five minutes.*

# Moses

## Nine-month-old English mastiff

I wish people wouldn't be afraid of me because of my size. I try very hard to be gentle, especially with kids—I adore kids. But the love of my life is Mom. I sleep with her, and she doesn't complain even when one of my feet ends up in her face. (Sorry about that, Mom, I don't do it on purpose.) I love to go in the car with her; once we drove all the way from Florida to New Hampshire. Being alone in a car like that is really quality time. Actually, I don't care where we are or what we're doing as long as we're together.

*The name mastiff, which comes from the word massive, actually refers to a family of very large dog breeds.*

*Enjoy being together*
*doing nothing at all.*

# Niko

## Eight-year-old French Briard

*This herding breed was used to keep sheep in unfenced areas. They were named for the French province of Brie, although this isn't believed to be their province of origin.*

Most days I go to work with Mom, a horse trainer. I never take my eyes off the kids during their lessons. When a rider falls, I'm the first one there. I lick her face until she responds, then I straddle her so she won't move until Mom says it's okay. At home I try to spend time with Dad since I don't see him during the day. If Dad sits on the sofa, I sit next to him. Like Dad, I put my butt on the couch and my feet on the floor. I help Mom, and I copy Dad to show them both how much I love them.

*Give him your heart.*

# Amber

## Eight-year-old shepherd mix

My favorite times are when I'm at home with my family, especially when we're touching in some way. It doesn't matter if it's my paw, my side, my head or all of me that's in contact with one of my humans, so long as there is some physical connection. I miss them when they go out, but I don't really mind being home alone because I'm surrounded by their smells. As much as I enjoy my own family, I'm not very social with other humans. I see other canines running up to strangers at the park, looking for attention, but I'd never do that. I only want affection from those I love.

*The American Kennel Club offers a Canine Good Citizen Program for mixed-breed dogs.*

*Enjoy casual touching.*

# Pugsley

## Five-year-old pug

My family consists of four people and three dogs. I enjoy playing with the other dogs. Our favorite game is tag. One of us starts to run, a second one chases, and the third one chases both of us. For some reason, Mom prefers that we do this outside. Even though I get along well with the other dogs, my strongest feelings are for the people in my family. I enjoy watching television with them, as long as I get cuddles or pets at the same time. Actually, anywhere I get cuddles is fine with me. I use my expressive face and wiggly body to communicate how much I love them.

*The breed name comes from the Latin word* pugnus, *which means fist, apparently referring to the shape of the dog's face.*

*Express your feelings
and emotions.*

# Maxie

## Two-year-old Airedale terrier

My first family didn't like my terrier personality. I now have a wonderful home with people who appreciate my intelligence, playful nature and outgoing disposition. I'm very interested in everything that's going on: When someone opens the refrigerator or closet door, I push my nose in to see what's happening. Through my inquisitive nature I have learned a lot.

*The breed is named for the area in which it originated, a valley in north-central England called Airedale.*

When I see my leash, that means we're going out, so I run to the front door and wait there. My cookies are kept in the pantry; when someone opens the pantry, I sit and wait for a treat. A pet or a hug means someone wants me to know I'm loved. That makes me happy!

*Let her know
she makes you happy.*

*When people talk, listen completely. Most people never listen.*

Ernest Hemingway

# communication

*No one appreciates the very special genius of your conversation as the dog does.*

Christopher Morley

# Queen Crystal

## Nickname Queenie, three-year-old Tibetan terrier

I tried to eat this photo—I'm sure you can understand why. I was definitely having a bad hair day. We had recently moved to a new house, and Mom was so busy getting us settled that she didn't have time for my daily brushing. Believe it or not, I'm actually a champion Tibetan terrier, so I'm used to looking my best. My brother, King Bentley, is also a champion. I'm not jealous when King scores higher than I do in the ring or when he gets attention from our humans. Attention from other canines? Now that is a different story.

*The Tibetan terrier is not a terrier; it was originally used as a herding dog, watchdog and companion dog by Tibetan monks.*

Don't take it out on him if you're having a bad hair day.

## sophie

**Five-year-old basset hound**

I got adopted after the Tri-County Humane Society in Boca Raton, Florida, put my picture in the newspaper. Mom saw it and rushed right over. The rest is history. I love being hugged and being close to my humans. I'm not allowed on the furniture, but I get around this to get my hugs by leaping on top of any family members sitting or lying on the furniture. When there's no one around, I like to lie in the sun; if there's a patch of sunshine anywhere in the house, I find it. The only thing that stresses me out is when a family member is upset or unhappy.

*The breed name comes from the French word* bas, *meaning low.*

Be sensitive to her feelings
and emotions.

# Leika

## Five-year-old German shepherd

My favorite toy is a tennis ball; I like carrying it around in my mouth, rolling it with my paw and playing fetch with it.

*These intelligent dogs were bred in Germany for herding; they patrolled the boundaries of an area to prevent animals, especially sheep, from entering or leaving.*

I enjoy going in the car, especially when the window is down and I can stick my head out. When we stop to get gas and I'm left alone in the car, I sit in the driver's seat. Too bad dogs can't drive—it looks like fun. My biggest thrill is obedience training. I like to learn new things and feel pride when I am able to understand what they want me to do. That's not easy, especially considering English is not my first language.

Try to understand
his point of view.

# Max

## Two-year-old Kerry blue terrier

My humans actually think they should be in charge! On the show circuit it's not an issue; I'm happy to take direction because I like doing well. I'm a Canadian champion and halfway to becoming an American champion. At home, it's another story. I have them trained to take me on long daily walks and jog with me at least once a week. Next, I want them to share their food. I've made it clear that I'm not satisfied with what's in my bowl by helping myself whenever they leave their food unattended. They yell when they catch me, and I bark when they yell. Hopefully they'll soon figure it out.

*Kerry blue terriers originated in Ireland in the mountainous region of County Kerry.*

*speak up about things
that are important to you.*

## Juliette

**Three-year-old shar-pei**

I was rescued from the Tri-County Humane Society in Boca Raton, Florida. My family consists of four wonderful people and two other dogs. I enjoy the other dogs and have fun playing with them, but we compete for attention. Fortunately, we have a lot of company so there's enough human attention to go around. Mom keeps life on a pretty tight schedule; with two kids and three dogs she probably has to!

*The Chinese shar-pei has been traced back to 200 B.C. through statues from that era, which depict these wrinkly dogs. In Chinese, shar-pei means sand skin.*

Being a creature of habit, I like having a schedule. Going off schedule—even in a small way like skipping a walk and being let into the yard instead—stresses me out. I stare at Mom to let her know I'm confused and concerned.

share your worries and concerns.

# Browser

## Six-month-old Jack Russell terrier

Obviously I don't have a real cell phone, but I wish I did—all this one does is make a dumb ringing sound when I bite it. But it would be truly wonderful if I could be in touch with my humans when they go out. When they're home, I'm totally responsive when they call me. Likewise when we're at the dog park, even if they interrupt my favorite pastime of chasing squirrels. When we leave the park before I'm ready, I grab one of my toys as soon as I get home and continue the game by keeping a tight grip and pretending it's a squirrel or another type of prey.

*The breed is named for John Russell, an Englishman who bred them as hunting dogs able to go underground to follow their quarry, usually a fox.*

*Be reachable when you're apart.*

# Gizmo

## Two-year-old long-haired Chihuahua

I love to go fishing. When my humans get the gear out, I stay close to make sure they don't forget me. In the boat, I lean over the side and bite at the fish. I jump and bark when they catch one. The only thing I don't like is how long it takes. And I get annoyed when they put the rods in a holder and relax with a beer. I take over then by standing on my hind legs and using my front paw to shake a rod; then I look to see if there's a fish. You see, I've figured out that the rod has to shake in order to get a fish.

*The breed is thought to have originated in Mexico during the Mayan period; chi in Mayan means dog.*

*Ask when you want something;*
*don't expect him to read your mind.*

# Yodel

## Four-year-old greater Swiss mountain dog

I like to learn new tricks—those I'm taught, such as roll over and give my paw, and those I learn on my own, like how to unlatch the back gate. I get hugs and treats for most tricks, but when I venture out the gate on my own, I get in trouble. Mom or Dad sits me down and lectures me about why I shouldn't do that. I bark my explanation, which is that I just want to patrol the perimeter of the house. I always come back when I'm done. Maybe if I can figure out how to latch the gate once I'm back they won't even know that I left.

*This breed is native to Switzerland; greater refers to the size of these dogs. They were used for guarding, herding and hauling.*

*Calmly discuss your differences.*

# Sophie

## Ten-month-old Pekingese

Mom and Dad say I'm perfect, and who am I to disagree? I think they're perfect too, and so is my life. I enjoy lying around in my dog beds (I have three). I like the action of the great outdoors, but when it's hot I'd rather just look out the window. I like other dogs, especially big

*For centuries, this breed could be owned only by members of the Chinese Imperial Palace.*

dogs; they're always curious when I wag my tail and roll onto my back. I like to sing and play dead because my humans enjoy it. The only thing I don't like is water. This includes rain, puddles and baths. I make my feelings known when anyone tries to make me get wet.

*share your true feelings.*

# Venus

## Three-year-old bulldog

Our last name isn't Williams, but my Lhasa apso sister and I are famous in our neighborhood. I am Venus, and she is Serena. Despite our size difference, Serena and I enjoy playing together. I lie on the floor while she races at, around and over me. Or I hold a rope toy while she tugs. When I've had enough I let her know by walking away; I get annoyed if she doesn't take the hint. I also get annoyed when Mom cleans between the wrinkles on my face. I know she means well, but I try to stop her by turning my face or pushing her hand away.

*The breed name refers to its original purpose in bullbaiting, a popular sport in the 1600s where bulldogs were trained to attack and kill bulls that were tied up.*

Give a warning when you're getting upset. It's better than holding back until you explode.

# Brooklyn

## Three-year-old mixed breed

Mom used to work at the Humane Society of Broward County, which is where I found her. I interviewed quite a few humans before I met her, and I'm glad I turned them all down because it was love at first sight with Mom! We are very compatible—we both enjoy chilling out at home, going for long walks and snuggling when we sleep. I love the way she talks to me as if we were the same species; I don't understand everything she says, but I know the words for most things that affect me. Sometimes all she needs is a sounding board, so I pay attention and try to look wise.

*Mixed-breed dogs are one-of-a-kind and are difficult, if not impossible, to duplicate.*

*Listen when she talks to you.*

# callaway

## Nickname Callie, eleven-year-old Shetland sheepdog

Mom is a horse trainer, and I usually go to work with her. When she's giving lessons, I join her and her students in the ring to make sure the horses go where they're supposed to go. (Mom and I don't always agree on where they're supposed to go, but that doesn't bother me, as I'm the one doing the herding.) I also don't get bothered when I am involved in an accident, like when a horse stepped on and broke my leg. Once it healed, I resumed my herding duties. When we're not working, Mom sometimes uses her training skills to teach me different tricks. Waving good-bye is my latest.

*The breed, also called Sheltie, originated in the Shetland Islands, rugged islands off the coast of Scotland. They were used to herd and guard sheep.*

*say good-bye nicely
when you part.*

# Dante

## Three-year-old Belgian Malinois

My dad is a canine behaviorist. He started training me when I was only twelve weeks old. My training has included obe-

*This sheepdog breed comes from the city of Malines, Belgium.*

dience, agility and personal protection work. Sometimes I help with his private training sessions by playing the role he assigns me: With aggressive dogs, I act assertive and dominant; with timid dogs, I act submissive to help build their confidence. When we're not working, we relax at home or do something fun. For example, Dad skates on his Rollerblades while I run next to him. If Dad's relaxing when I want to run, I go bark at his Rollerblades. If Dad doesn't notice when it's walk time, I bring him my leash.

*Be clear about your needs.*

# Sam

## Six-month-old Dandie Dinmont

When I was young, I was left at a veterinarian's office. I spent several days in a cage, where I passed the time looking at the canines that came and went with their humans. Then I saw a beautiful girl—I've since learned that she's a Tibetan spaniel. I started jumping and calling her. Her mom looked at me and then talked to one of the employees. The next thing I knew, I was in the car with them. I'm a happy boy now and play constantly with my girlfriend and our mom. The only thing that makes me unhappy is being separated from either one of them.

*Dandie Dinmont was a character in Sir Walter Scott's novel* Guy Mannering. *He had a pack of terriers indigenous to the area of Scotland in which the book is set.*

*Let her know you'll miss her
when she travels without you.*

# calí

## Six-month-old boglen terrier

I share my home with an older bossy canine. Usually I let her get away with it; when I don't, I try to avoid a confrontation. For example, if I have a bone I want to save for later, I sneak off and bury it— a favorite place is between the cushions on the couch. Another example is bedtime. We both sleep with our humans, and she lets me know I belong at the foot of the bed. So I lie there until she falls asleep; then I move up and put my head on the pillow. When I need help dealing with her, I give one of my humans "the look."

*A boglen terrier is a hybrid between a Boston terrier and a beagle; other names for this mix are poogle and peagle.*

Let him know when something is
wrong, without whining or nagging.

# Murphy

## Eight-year-old Portuguese water dog

As a working breed, I'm happy to have a mom who is a dog trainer and gives me the responsibility of helping with her classes. I help show her human students how to communicate with their canines, and her canine students what they should do. Mom has also taught me a lot of advanced tricks. My personal favorite is when she tells me to go night-night. I get into my bed and pull a blanket over myself.

*The breed was used by fishermen in the coastal areas of Portugal to herd fish into nets, retrieve anything that fell into the water and carry messages between ships.*

When I demonstrate this, people always say "Aww . . ." Mom's favorite is when she tells me to say I'm sorry. I bow down and give her an apologetic look.

134

*Apologize when you're wrong or when you cause hurt feelings.*

# Freddy

## Eleven-year-old Bedlington terrier

My American Kennel Club name is Frederick von Lamb Chop. I'm not sure if this refers to my appearance or my gentle disposition; both are fitting. I've never met a person or a dog I didn't like, although I prefer people and feel I have more in common with them than with my own species. People are also the source of things I enjoy most: car rides, belly rubs and chicken. I don't mean to brag, but I recently appeared in several TV commercials for our family business. Dad thinks people remember the commercials because of the clever lyrics he wrote, and I'd never hurt his feelings by letting on that I'm what makes them memorable.

*The breed originated in England and was named after the mining shire of Bedlington.*

*Be gentle with issues
that involve his ego.*

*If you judge people, you have no time to love them.*

Mother Teresa

# Acceptance

*Animals are such agreeable friends—they ask no questions, they pass no criticisms.*

George Eliot

# oliver

## Seven-year-old bearded collie

In the tradition of my breed, I go to work every day with Mom. She owns a trendy women's clothing store where I am responsible for greeting our employees and customers. I believe in making work fun for everyone, so I listen for the delivery trucks that pull up at the back door and when I hear one, I race to the door, jump up and use my paws to open it. My human friends seem to enjoy it, and I get to stretch my legs a bit. At home, my favorite place to hang out is the shower stall—don't ask!

*Bearded collies got their name because the long hair that flows from their chin to their chest looks like a beard.*

Be patient when
you go shopping with her.

# charlie

## Fifteen-month-old mixed breed

My dad adopted me from the Humane Society of Broward
County in Fort Lauderdale, Florida. Sometimes I think
we're like *The Odd Couple*. He's rather per-
snickety about keeping things neat, while
I sometimes make a mess, especially when
I'm home alone. I especially like unrolling
toilet paper. I grab one end in my mouth and run around
the house until the roll is empty. Then I chew some of it into
tiny pieces. Dad doesn't yell, but he cleans it up right away,
which usually requires taking out the vacuum for the little
pieces. I hate that thing—it's way too loud. But there's no
stopping Dad when he decides something needs to be done.

*Mixed-breed dogs are
usually the result of
"unplanned pregnancies."*

*Accept that you don't have to be the alpha.*

# ziggie

## Seventeen-month-old puggle

I'm a very easygoing guy—I love other dogs, people and even cats. I spend a lot of time with my family, but I also make friends with people everywhere we go. I get to spend a lot of time with other dogs; I usually see several dogs on my walks, plus I have regular playdates with one dog friend. I don't spend much time with cats; for some reason, cats usually run away when I approach them. When left on my own, my favorite pastime is stealing Mom's shoes. Fortunately she's pretty easygoing, too, and doesn't seem to mind—unless I chew on them.

*A puggle is a mix between a pug and a beagle.*

*Don't sweat the small stuff.*

# Gracie

## Three-year-old mixed breed

I'm quite a flexible girl; I learned to be at an early age, as I lived in four different homes before I was a year old.

*In England, mixed-breed dogs are called mongrels. In the United States, mutt is a more acceptable term and mongrel is considered derogatory.*

Although I had some bad experiences, each time I went to a new family I did everything I could to show my love and to earn theirs. When Mom adopted me, I finally found the love I had been looking for. She and I have great times together.

My favorite place to be is outside, walking the neighborhood or going to the dog park. No matter where I am, I socialize with everyone, whether they have two legs or four.

*Allow yourself to*
*be vulnerable.*

# Sidney

## Ten-month-old Labrador retriever

Luna is my best canine friend in the whole world; we meet regularly at the dog park with other members of our play group. Sometimes our moms get the two of us together at one of our houses.

*The breed originated in Newfoundland, Canada, where it was originally called a small Newfoundland. The breed was refined in England and the name was changed to Labrador retriever.*

# Luna

## Sixteen-month-old Labrador retriever

My three favorite things are eating carrots, swimming and seeing my friends—both canine and human. Sidney is my best canine friend; our Moms, who are also friends, introduced us. I've never met a dog I didn't like.

Have your own friends
and understand that he needs
his own friends.

# Ginger

## Twelve-year-old Alaskan malamute

It doesn't take much to make me happy, as I am well taken care of by two loving people. If I need anything, I just let them know and they provide it. If my water dish is empty, I say "wa wa" and bring them my empty dish—of course they fill it up right away. When I'm not feeling well they give me special food. I can't jump on the furniture anymore, so they have a dog bed in every room for my convenience. I spend most of my time lying on one of the beds, napping or just chilling out.

*The breed originated with the Mahlemiut tribe in Northwestern Alaska for whom it is named. They were used during the Alaska Gold Rush to pull heavy loads.*

Be content to spend
quiet time at home.

# Ghetto

## Fifteen-month-old mixed breed

I was brought to a vet after I was hit by a car, a painful experience, I assure you. The vet was incredible; he did so much for me, although one thing he couldn't do was save my leg. But I get along just fine on three legs. I am able to walk without a problem, and I can even run. Not only did the vet save my life, but I actually *got* a life when one of his employees became my mom. Now I have a wonderful home, a family and lots of friends, both human and canine.

*Many dogs that end up at shelters have special needs, physical and/or emotional. Once these needs are met, they can become incredibly loyal, loving pets.*

*Don't let adversity
sour your outlook.*

# Ahab

## Three-month-old shih tzu

Mom is a photographer—*the* photographer for this book! Dad's a yacht captain, which is how I got my name, and how our cat got the name Nemo. I wonder what they'd name a baby. Hook? Queeg? Just joking. I'm not complaining about my name; I think it's very cool. Mom and Dad are very cool, too. They take good care of me, and I know they always will. They give me an amazing amount of attention, but they lead busy lives, so sometimes I have to entertain myself. Fortunately, I have a collection of balls, some of which are quite unusual. Mom says I'm obsessed with them, but that's an exaggeration.

*Shih tzu comes from the Chinese word for lion; this name was given to the breed because of their long, flowing mane-like coat.*

*Trust him with your life.*

# Rocky

## Seven-year-old rottweiler

I'm sure you've heard of the *Rocky* movies (what great theme music!). I don't know why they named these movies after me—I don't believe in fighting. That doesn't mean I like everything that happens to me: I didn't like being abused in my first home, and after I was adopted by my wonderful family I wasn't happy when the boys left for college. But I'm good at adapting. Once the boys left, Mom became my major responsibility. We have a lot of guests, probably because Mom has a home-based business. I greet them enthusiastically. When they leave, I bark ferociously to make sure Mom knows they're leaving and that it's okay.

*The breed is descended from ancient Roman herding dogs. It is named for the German town of Rottweil.*

156

*Resist the urge to spar.*

# Sydney

## Four-year-old blue heeler Australian cattle dog

When I was seven months old, my family adopted me from outside a pet store. I was very happy to have a home, but there were two issues that had to be resolved before I could settle in. The first was that they had a cat named Hobbes. And Hobbes got lots of attention. Second, they wanted me to wear a leash. I never wore one before and I did not like it one bit. Mom tricked me into cooperating with the leash by putting it on Hobbes and praising him. I fell for it and learned to walk on a leash; I've even learned to get along with Hobbes.

*The breed was developed in Australia to help farmers herd cattle that range over vast land areas.*

Be nice to her cat, even if
you don't like cats.

# Daní

## Eighteen-month-old miniature pinscher (min pin)

My favorite place is the dog park. I may be small in stature but I'm not a foo-foo, small-dog type, so I like to hang out

*The miniature pinscher is not a scaled-down version of the Doberman pinscher. In German, pinscher means biter and refers to dogs that jump on and bite their quarry.*

with the big dogs. We sniff each other, roll in the grass, chase balls, bark, run in a pack, chase each other and pretend to attack. I particularly enjoy pretend attacks, especially with dogs much bigger than I am. My humans get nuts when that happens; they scold me and tell me I have a Napoleonic complex. They obviously don't get it! It's about knowing when to take a stand and when to give in.

*Expect some power struggles,*
*and that you won't always win.*

# Laurelei

## One-year-old American Eskimo dog

I spent time wandering the streets before I was picked up by a nice lady who became my foster mom. She bathed me to get rid of my fleas and ticks, and took care of me until I started to gain weight. Then she found me a home with two wonderful dads. They actually wanted a girl, and even though I'm a guy, they gave me the name they'd already picked out. It took a little getting used to, but I've grown to like

*The breed became known as the American Eskimo when it was first registered with the American Kennel Club by a couple whose kennel was named American Eskimo.*

it. Even if I didn't like it, it wouldn't matter, because in the scheme of things, it's not important. I love my dads, and they love me.

Be prepared to weather storms
in your relationship.

# Tyler

## Five-year-old bichon frise

I'm a happy-go-lucky guy. What's not to like about my life? Mom is beautiful, on the inside as well as the outside. Dad is good to both of us. I don't have to share them with other animals, or—perish the thought—children. With Mom I love to cuddle; with Dad I love to play. My favorite game is when Dad tosses a treat: I jump up and catch it midair. My favorite part of the day is dinner, because we have quality family time. The three of us sit at the dining room table. On good days I get leftovers; otherwise I eat my regular food.

*The breed originated in the Mediterranean and was originally called the barbichon, later shortened to bichon. The French added the word* frise, *which refers to its soft curly hair.*

Don't complain about the food,
even if it seems to be the same
thing day in and day out.

# wilhelmina

## Nickname Willie, six-year-old dachshund

I have two favorite hobbies, and I'm not sure which I prefer. I love to hunt lizards and I love to roll in things that smell bad. I can combine the two when I find a dead lizard, preferably one that isn't newly dead. Mom and Dad didn't seem to mind all that much, until recently, when they had a baby. Now they get upset when I bring my special smells inside. The baby has really changed our lives. On the minus side, it's a lot noisier in our house, yet I'm supposed to be more quiet. But on the plus side, it's amazing the gifts I get when they're feeling guilty.

*The breed comes from Germany where the name means badger dog. Dachshunds were bred to hunt and kill badgers.*

166

Accept the jewelry he
gives you as a token of his love.

# willie

## Three-year-old Nova Scotia duck tolling retriever

Next month I'm going to the Westminster Kennel Club Dog Show, an honor that comes with a lot of responsibility. Most people have no idea what goes on behind the scenes, much less what it takes to get there. But they also don't understand how it feels to be out in that ring, adrenaline rushing as you compete. So I work hard, respect my handler, and put up with all the bathing, brushing and primping for my chance to shine. (This seemed an affront to my masculinity until I saw other males enduring the same things.) It is very, very intense. After a show I'm glad to go home, where I can relax and just be me.

*Tolling is a Middle English word that means to entice. These retrievers were bred to lure ducks closer to the hunters.*

Sometimes the best thing
to do is grin and bear it.

# Charley Frances

## Seven-month-old cockapoo

I'm a very social girl, with people and also others of my species. When we go on walks I like to stop and sniff hello to every canine we see. I even have a boyfriend, a black mixed breed; our moms arrange play-dates for us and we have a great time. My favorite people are the children in the family. I also love to play with

*The breed, a hybrid between a cocker spaniel and a poodle, originated in the United States in the 1950s.*

them, although it is sure different than playing with my guy. Usually they're gentle with me; when they do get rough, I just walk away. I've learned that things aren't always the way I want them to be, and it isn't worth getting upset.

*Don't complain if he keeps
the house too cold for you;
just put on a sweater.*

# Jessie

## Six-month old English cocker spaniel

I believe in speaking up for myself, to say I want something I don't have or I don't want to do something I've been asked

*This breed is larger than the American cocker spaniel— which was developed from the English cocker spaniel. The English spaniel also has a longer muzzle and a larger head.*

to do. I'm not loud like our neighbor who constantly makes those shrill, piercing barks that drive me crazy. I just make soft little woof sounds to express my feelings. I love people, especially my family. When they're home, I follow them wherever they go, looking for attention. When they're either out or busy, I am quite capable of amusing myself. I enjoy chewing on my bones, my toys or anything else that's handy.

Find ways to entertain
yourself when she's busy.

# Sophie

## Nine-month-old Tibetan spaniel

I began my life in a puppy mill that was so crowded I didn't have room to walk. I was rescued and taken to the Tri-County Humane Society in Boca Raton, Florida. They nursed me back to health, taught me how to walk and found me a wonderful home. Everything about my life is new and different, but in a good way. For example, they give me a lot of toys, and some of them make unusual noises. Part of the fun is not knowing what to expect. That's actually my philosophy of life. Perhaps because I started out with nothing to look forward to, I now enjoy whatever comes my way.

*Despite the name, this breed is not a true spaniel. Spaniels were gun dogs, while Tibetan spaniels were bred by Buddhist monks in Tibet to be watchdogs.*

*Accept that there will be times
when the opposite sex
is a mystery to you.*

*It is not the failure of others to appreciate your abil-ities that should trouble you, but rather your failure to appreciate theirs.*

Confucius

# Appreciation

*My goal in life is to be as good a person as my dog already thinks I am.*

Author unknown

# Keri

## Show name Shorlyne Sunspyte Merry Cartel, six-year-old Welsh terrier

When I'm in my show mode, I focus on doing my best. It's a stimulating environment, and sometimes I almost quiver with excitement. But I have to contain myself and act appropriately. When we return home, I need to use all that energy I have stored up. I enjoy hunting the lizards, squirrels and rabbits in our yard; I try to run my prey to the ground. I enjoy just being outside; when I'm not hunting I like to lie in the sun. I also enjoy going for walks—the longer the better. Inside, I enjoy playing with squeaky toys and chewing ice cubes. But most of all, I enjoy being with my mom.

*Welsh terriers originated in Wales, where they were bred to hunt foxes, badgers and otters.*

*Show her that she brings you joy.*

# Don Juan

## Nickname D.J., two-year-old mixed breed

I got my name at the Humane Society because I have such a loveable nature. But after my adoption, Dad felt self-conscious because people stared and laughed when they heard him call me. That's why I got a nickname. It's a cool nickname, but personally I think Don Juan is more fitting because my favorite thing to do is kiss. My second favorite thing to do is chase the ducks at the pond. (In case you're wondering, I have no interest in kissing the ducks.) I let Dad know how much I love to go to the pond by giving him a big smile when he takes me there.

*With some mixed breeds, it's fairly easy to identify their breed origins. Those that aren't easy to identify are sometimes called a "Heinz 57" variety.*

*smile to show your approval.*

# Bacardí

## Twelve-year-old cocker spaniel

My happiest times are when the grandchildren visit, because I get lots of attention. They usually stay less than a week, so I make the most of every minute. When they leave the house, I take my nap by the door; this way I know as soon as they return. My least favorite thing is taking a bath; when I see a hair dryer, I hide under the bed. Once it's over, I'm happy because the brushing part feels soooo good. It also feels good to be clean and to get a clean scarf. My favorites are the holiday-themed ones because they show that I'm included in the festivities.

*The breed originated in America and is also known as the American cocker spaniel. It was originally bred to hunt woodcock, thus the name cocker spaniel.*

Let her know you enjoy and
appreciate it when she pampers you.

# Bennet

## Six-year-old Pembroke Welsh corgi

I live with my biological brother, Dominick. It's wonderful to have someone to play with, especially when we're home alone. We chase each other around the house. Dominick likes to leap on and off the furniture; I like to weave under it—so we do both. Sometimes we accidentally knock things over, and we know we're going to get into trouble. So we listen for the door to open, and then we roll over on our backs with all four feet in the air. That's our way of saying we're sorry and please don't be mad. We hate it when our humans are mad at us; we never get mad at them.

*There are two types of Welsh corgis: the Cardigan and the Pembroke. The Pembroke Welsh corgi, the one without a tail, is the favorite dog of Queen Elizabeth II.*

Look at him through
rose-colored glasses.

# Duchess

## Nine-year-old collie

Not only do I love my family, but I'm also grateful to them for rescuing me. I let them know how I feel by giving them affection, devotion and complete loyalty, and by being in a good mood whenever we're together. I am quite laid back, except when my services are needed. When the doorbell rings, I bark to announce that there's a guard dog on duty. When the telephone rings, I use my nose to knock it off the hook, then I bark. After that, I'm not sure what to do. When I'm in a group of people or animals, I use my herding skills to keep them together.

*The breed originated in Scotland and is thought to be named for the breed of sheep it once herded, colley sheep.*

*Let him know how happy
you are that he's in your life.*

# Rambo

## One-year-old West Highland terrier (Westie)

I may be small in stature, but don't let my size mislead you.
I'm a serious guard dog with a big deep bark. My bark is so
intimidating that I've never had to
follow it with any action. I consider
myself to be on duty 24/7; with my
keen sense of hearing, it's easy. My
humans tease me about my barking; they say I even bark in my sleep.
If that's true (and I'm not admitting it is), they shouldn't
complain because their sleep noises aren't exactly pleasing.
My humans also tease me about my appetite; but, hey, I'm a
growing boy. When they feed me something special, I woof
my appreciation.

*The breed originated
in Poltalloch, Scotland
and was originally called
the Poltalloch terrier.*

*compliment the chef.*

# zoey

## Nickname Gator, fourteen-month-old St. Bernard

To entertain myself, I carry my tennis ball to the top of the stairs, nudge it with my nose and race it down. Then I go back to the top and start all over again. When I get tired, I take a nap in my favorite place to sleep: our Roman tub. If one of my humans wants to take a bath, they expect me to move even if I've staked my claim and I'm sound asleep. I can't understand why they like to sit in a tub of water or how they think that this is a good way to get clean; personally, I prefer a shower.

*The breed name comes from the work these dogs did rescuing travelers crossing the treacherous passes through the Alps between Switzerland and Italy, specifically the pass known as Saint Bernard Pass.*

Let him know you appreciate being
treated to a day at the spa.

# Kiley

## Six-year-old toy fox terrier

As you can see, I don't have much fur. So I'm always cold, and finding ways to get warm is a top priority. At night it's pretty easy; I just burrow under the covers. During the day, I like to be under the "binkie" that I've had since I was adopted. I have my humans trained to put my binkie over me whenever I bring it to them. I also have sweaters that I sometimes wear. I like them okay, but they don't cover all of me. Still, I think it's sweet when they get me a new one, so I act happy even though it's less exciting than a new toy.

*As the name implies, this breed was created to hunt foxes. They originated in England, with the toy version originating in the United States.*

*Enjoy it if he spoils you,*
*but don't act spoiled.*

# Ralph

## Eight-year-old Chihuahua

My second favorite thing is food. My humans call me their piglet; I would be insulted, except they say it affectionately, and I do love to eat. I especially like anything they're having: vegetables, fruits, meat, crackers—it's all more tasty than dog food. (If they ever tried that stuff I don't think they would feed it to me anymore!) My favorite thing is snuggling; 24 hours a day would suit me fine. When Mom sits or lies down, I climb in her lap or lie down with my body against hers. When she's standing up, I give her my special look to let her know I want to be close.

*This is the smallest pedigreed pooch in the world. It is believed to have lived in the wild before being captured and domesticated.*

*Let her know you find her appealing.*

# Blackjack

## Eight-year-old toy poodle

The pack I live with consists of two humans and three other canines. I consider myself to be the pack leader. I let them know what I want them to do, then I growl if they don't do it. For example, to let Dad know it's time to go out, I pace back and forth. If he doesn't take me out, I scratch on his legs. If he still doesn't take me out, that's when I growl. I also let my pack members know when they do something that pleases me. For example, when I get a new toy or a bone, I hold it in my mouth to show I like it.

*In France, the breed is called* caniche, *which comes from* canichon. *A canichon is a baby duck that hasn't gotten its mature feathers yet.*

Thank him when he
gives you a gift.

# Pooh

## Seven-month-old French bulldog

Like a lot of guys, I put up a tough front, but inside I'm quite the opposite. I cover up my soft side in different ways. Sometimes I try to make my humans laugh by doing something goofy like chasing my tail. Sometimes I bark loudly and jump up and down. Sometimes I pout and go under the bed or turn my back. All of these behaviors are distractions to cover up my real feelings. But the bottom line is I need the people in my life, especially Mom. I don't know what I'd do without her.

*The breed was derived from a miniature version of the English bulldog, which was imported to France, bred with a French terrier and named the French bulldog.*

Imagine how lonely your life
would be without her in it.

# Quincy

## Three-year-old Yorkshire terrier

My brother Zack and I belong to the author of this book (actually, she belongs to us). I have to admit that she spoils us. I love my toys, especially what I call my ducky, even though it's actually a pheasant. I have three identical duckies; at night I can't sleep unless my entire flock is in bed with us. But as important as my duckies are to me, and as much as I like having lots of toys, the love I get from my family is much more important. I know I am one of the luckiest dogs in the world because of the love we have for each other.

*Yorkies became an official breed in 1870 after an English reporter stated, "They ought no longer to be called Scotch Terriers, but Yorkshire Terriers for having been so improved here."*

Realize that the people
in your life are more important
than your possessions.

# Benji

## Two-year-old silky terrier

I may not look it, but I'm a very independent guy. Just because I'm small enough to be picked up doesn't mean I like to be (unless it's my idea, of course). I also don't like being taken to the vet when there's nothing wrong with me—I don't appreciate the shots they give me every year. When I'm sick, that's different.

*The breed originated in Australia, where it is known as the Australian silky terrier. Silky refers to its soft coat.*

I hate to admit, it but it scares me, because I don't know what's the matter or how long it's going to last or how to make it better. Then I do need help and maybe a trip to the dreaded vet (where I sit in Mom's lap for reassurance).

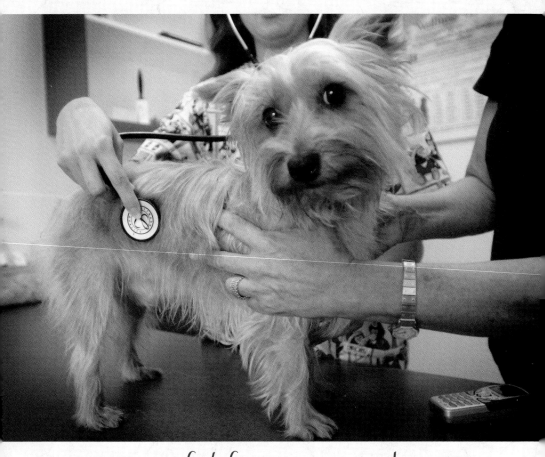

Be grateful for support when
you have health problems.

# Max

## Ten-year-old beagle

My family consists of two humans and my lady friend, Minnie, another beagle. I couldn't ask for a better canine companion, although it wouldn't hurt her to lose a few pounds. Of course, she could say the same about me! Our humans are absolutely wonderful; we try to show them how much we love them, and they give us lots of love. They also give each other lots of love (I won't go into details), but sometimes they do argue. I can't stand it when they raise their voices, so whenever they argue I position myself between them to act as peacemaker. This has earned me the nickname "the Marriage Counselor."

*Beagles originated in England. The breed name is thought to have come from the Old English word* beag, *meaning small.*

*Let him know you
think he's wonderful.*

# Hart

## Four-year-old kooikerhondje

My humans say that the nickname for my breed—kook—is perfect for me, because I'm always entertaining. They get a special kick out of the way I run with a toy, then fling it in the air and pounce on it. I especially enjoy doing this with toys that talk when banged on the floor. I love being outside where there is room to run; I usually hold a toy in my mouth as I run. My humans seem to think that means I want to play fetch, so sometimes I accommodate them; but I'm just as happy playing on my own.

*This Dutch breed was used as a decoy dog by duck hunters. The breed name comes from the word* eendenkooi, *which means decoy dog.*

Find joy in the simple things.

## Lulu

**Five-year-old mixed breed**

At a young age I ended up in a shelter in San Juan, Puerto Rico; from there I was sent to a shelter in the U.S., where I was lucky to be adopted right away. It's hard to describe what it's like to have your first real home. There's no more hunger, no more loneliness, no more fear. And what a set-up! Carpeting to scratch my back on, soft furniture to relax on, a real bed to sleep in. I have all these toys, too, and I get to go to the dog park to play with other dogs. The best part of my life is that I am living it with Mom.

*Some dog clubs use the term all-American as the breed name for mixed breeds or mutts. This refers to the United States' population, a mixture of people from different countries, cultures and races.*

Take time to enjoy your
relationship; it's a journey,
not a destination.

# Acknowledgments

Thanks to Amy Hill for the beautiful photography, and for the fun we had along the way. Thanks to all the dog owners who generously allowed us to photograph their dogs—and to those who agreed to appear in the photos with their dogs. I regret that every dog's photo couldn't be used, and I hope the owners of those that aren't included understand.

To all the people who were kind enough to recommend dogs for inclusion in this book, thanks for making it possible to have so many different breeds. Special thanks to Diane Basel of the Boca Raton Dog Club, who worked with me over time and was so helpful in finding unusual breeds.

To my literary attorney, David Koehser, thank you for your guidance and patience. To Iain Calder, author of *The Untold Story: My 20 Years Running the National Enquirer,* thanks for taking the time to provide encouragement and support to a neighbor.

My deepest appreciation to the entire staff of Health Communications Inc., for the final outcome of this book and for our collaborative working relationship. Special appreciation to the following HCI people: Theresa Peluso for going well beyond her assigned responsibilities and for providing invaluable mentoring and advice; to Michele Matrisciani, Andrea Gold and the rest of the editorial staff for their dedication and attention to detail; to Larissa Henoch for caring so much about the layout and design; to Pat Holdsworth for the many hats she wears and for all her support; and to Peter Vegso for taking a chance on me.

I am also grateful to my family for being there for me throughout this process, especially my brother Lee, for encouraging—even nagging—me to move forward on the book; my sister, Frances, and my brother George, for their ongoing feedback and advice; my husband, Richard, and my daughter, Laura, for understanding when I was preoccupied; and my dogs, Zack and Quincy, for dealing with all the dog smells I wore after each photography session.

# Author

**Carla Genender** is the former president of a "boutique" management consulting company serving Fortune 500 companies. Many of her projects involved interpersonal relationships. Carla is a qualified practitioner of the Myers-Briggs Personality Types Instrument, and has developed numerous corporate initiatives to help professionals interact better with others. She has been a dog lover since the age of five when a cocker spaniel adopted her family. She has had Yorkshire terriers since graduating from college. As an observer and participant of both human/human and human/canine relationships, she came to realize that dogs often seem better at relationships than humans. She lives in Boca Raton, Florida, with her husband, Richard; and two Yorkies, Zack and Quincy. Her daughter, Laura, is a student at Sweetbriar College.

# Photographer

**Amy Hill** graduated magna cum laude from the Art Institute of Fort Lauderdale. She began her career as a stringer (part-time photographer) for the Miami Herald and assisted professional photographers in many specialty areas. During this time, she developed a passion for documenting weddings, and became a wedding photographer. Amy's photographs throughout the book reflect her passion for dogs as well as her sensitivity and creativity. Amy and her husband, David, live in Fort Lauderdale, Florida, with their shih tzu, Ahab, and cat, Nemo.

Photo by Migel Irias

# Cover Dogs

## Champ
**Seven-year-old golden retriever (left)**

I'm a pet therapy dog for the Humane Society of Broward County in Fort Lauderdale, Florida. I enjoy my visits to hospitals and feel good that I am able to provide comfort to patients, families and nurses. I also visit local schools—sometimes the children read to me, and even children who don't like to read get excited when they're reading to me! When I'm not working, I'm a beach boy. I love to swim in the ocean, chase fish and bask in the attention I usually get.

## Gracie
**Three-year-old golden retriever (right)**

I'm also a pet therapy dog for the Humane Society of Broward County. My specialty is working with children in hospitals. It's very rewarding to help out and know that while the children are busy petting and hugging me, they don't seem to be aware of the chemo and other treatments they're receiving. I also work with children at rehabilitation centers, and I visit boys and girls clubs. When I'm not working, I know how to use my femininity to get what I want and to keep guys like Champ in line.